FABER NEW

IN THE SAME SERIES

Tom Warner

faber and faber

First published in 2010
by Faber and Faber Ltd
Bloomsbury House
74–77 Great Russell Street
London WC1B 3DA

Typeset by Faber & Faber Ltd
Printed in England by T. J. International Ltd, Padstow, Cornwall

ACKNOWLEDGEMENTS

Thanks are due to the editors of *The Rialto, Smiths Knoll, Stand*
and *10th Muse* and Gatehouse Press, to the Society of Authors
for an Eric Gregory Award and to George Szirtes,
my family and Laura.

A CIP record for this book
is available from the British Library

ISBN 978-0-571-25002-8

2 4 6 8 10 9 7 5 3 1

Contents

Sunlight and Rain

They drove in silence
and brightness of dawn.

They drove in the strobe
of dawn bright in trees.

They drove in brightness
through brightness

into a whale like a storm
like clouds humped black
at the motorway's end.

They drove in silence
and brightness
and blackness
into a whale
into rain as fat as pennies

into the white noise of rain
as fat as pennies
into the static fuzz of rain
and brightness
where flyovers were gasps
in the white noise of rain as fat as pennies
gobfuls of air
grabbed in the grapple of drowning
in the white noise fuzz
of rain as fat as pennies.

They drove in silence
over miles of worn pelts and feather

flattened beneath a black anvil of cloud.
They drove in silence and rain

through silver pennies
and smudged pelts
into the gape of a whale

and a crushed wing
lifted in their windy wake

turn around
come back.

History

O loved one, better you're not mentioned in poems.
Better your name appears in no shifting library.

Let's leave history well alone to level
cities to monochromic rubble

to its harvesting, to barns of human hair
and unclaimed names.

Plates drift and collide.
The piled volcanoes of histories darken.

Let's lie together where we end, tired and heavy
as a cow falling to her shins in the heat.

Bricks. Mortar.

The spider we watched beyond the pane is still there,
in the pyracantha, despite the windy months.
Patient, fat as a bull's-eye among its glassy spokes,
until a bird picks it off.

Perhaps the greatest thing we did
was toss an apple core from a car,
tumbling into miles of soft verges,

or trap a red admiral in the shell of our four hands
and bear its weight to an open window.

Under *Natural History*

every mushroom-picking pocket book I find
contains some kind of disclaimer.

Collecting mushrooms to eat is dangerous.
No field guide is ever comprehensive.

So I bought two, and slung them in a rattan basket.
The kind of basket some of the girls at school

would nurse from Home Ec. in the crook of their elbows.
The kind of girls, like Suzanne Galloway, with thick tights

who sometimes carried violins in rigid cases
for lunchtime sessions in the music block.

All welcome.
Open. Optional. Twelve o'clock.

Once, Brett Coupe pulled the heavy doors open wide enough
for us to peer in at girls standing without their blazers,

violins trapped beneath their chins like telephones or windy babies,
and at their feet were cases filled with satin and crushed velvet.

I kick my boots clean outside and leave them at the door.
On the kitchen table I drop a basket full of mushrooms,

some red as blood, some purple and crinkly-edged
some squishy cups like orange water lilies.

I'm pretty sure this one's an Amethyst Deceiver.
You ask me why I'd take that risk, but I can't really answer.

Astacology

Astacology is the study of crayfish
and won't get past Microsoft's spell-check.

Crayfish, also known as
crodgers, crawdaddies, mudbugs and yabbies.

The one I found among the crabby rocks
of a disused mill was a crawdaddy, laden with eggs.

I pinched her, finger and thumb, across the cephalothorax;
a spiny tongue, severed, snapping and flicking.

I thought of the awkward American girl with large teeth
who corrected my pronunciation of Los Angeles.

Lost and Found

Kitten. Cat. An English bull terrier. A peach-faced lovebird,
one of a pair. More lost than found. No budgies or *budgerigars*.

We took it to be good fortune that he was blown in from wherever
to precisely here, a strange fruit in the cherry blossom tree.

We took it to be a windfall that he alighted lightly on our lives
on this cloudless Pentecost. We were good and meant good.

By dusk, as elsewhere rooks hang their black on the last light,
something falls on us like responsibility or a beetling guilt.

Rain softens notes taped to phone boxes, telegraph poles,
bus shelters. *Found. Budgie.* In the dark and the rain, a name,

given flippantly, only ever meant to be temporary, solidifies:
Alcatraz.

Mole

Perfect; last night's velvet purse, with clumsy clasps,
carelessly dropped by arms wrapped in arms.
Or, kneeling closer, the barrel-bodied hostess in her fur coat,
her mouth relaxed to a smudge of rouge,
repugnant, sleeping off the garden party in the garden.

I once found four. Four in a row on a barbed-wire fence,
each snagged through the skull and left to hang,
their pelts to slough away to nothing more
than an owl might cough up in the filthy nest.
With clawed gloves outspread, they were scarecrows, or scales.
Little men, starved and stretched, crucified
there on the hill's curved spine;
four crosses, four signposts with their eight stony ways.

Back along the path, the mole is gone.
The lush has stirred from her stupor; the purse is found
by the returning lover before she even missed it.
Perhaps the sun breathed into the mole, filling his pockets
until they swelled and breathed back.
Perhaps he's rolling again the massed earth beneath him.

Easter

All week, warily direct,
she pecked leaf litter,
shook out soft nesting
to line the tatty cup in our hedge.

And now,
in the dark of thorns, motionless,
she no longer breaks cover as I pass
or stand and look down on her;

the colour of her bowl,
except for the yellow beak
and corona
of her unblinking eye.

I might have slid my hands
between the thorns,
together in prayer or a dive,
cradled her light boat,

eggs, her,
like an ounce of water,
crept them through the stony garden
and climbed them higher.

Rabbit

He has a recurring dream
in which he's a rabbit;
the familiar black night,
the narrow track
which he must cross.
His rabbit-heart is furious,
terrified.

He starts forward, but his fat rear
flops unwillingly.
The hill's ridge begins to glow,
burns.
Two lights break their dawns
then dip towards him,
like god-eyes.

He never dreams of the room
with a single window
which he's never seen.
He hasn't dreamed
the seagulls kiting against the wind
as the wind charges over fields
but isn't heard through the glass.

Wisteria

has reached our window.

Insidious, advancing in imperceptible shudders,
spiralling the sunflower's stake. We hadn't noticed
until it spread a question at the window,
and rolled out a reddening arm towards the doorstep.

My grandfather is in the hospital,
my father is older than I thought.

I could hack it back.

The Fathomless

Down here the seagull's wing holds no wind;
a fist of quills, a sandy shuttlecock remnant.
Vast in leafy pools, crabs await
the tide, or, soft-shelled, clasp themselves
in salty hollows below the smoothed groynes.
Sand fleas break about the tide line's wreckage;
sorted lines of shingle, and broken traps.

Son of Modern Man, measure yourself
against the cliff, the monumental strata.

Minutia. You might have been a sea anemone,
an eyed plum. You, swollen with blood.

Climb the weft with bloody fingers,
with chalk-dry feet and cracked nails in the warp,
to bed down on your stratum of windy grass.

Under the Moon

In a shanty town of chimneys and aerials,
plumped pigeons roost their silhouettes.
Under the pigeons, children sleep with their pets
in rooms stencilled with bright fairy-sentinels.
Under the children, parents wipe surfaces
and watch television. A windless snowfall
corrects typing errors; streets like rows of kisses.
But disasters *have* happened, are happening, *will*.
Under the parents, the unmentioned monsters
that slam doors are tonight locked down in the cellars.
The children are hurt. O mothers, fathers!
They are lying at school, and they don't tell us.
The morning snow has made grottoes of the cars.
A blackbird stitches the front lawn with scars.

Mr Kinder Collecting Apples

They say you shouldn't climb a ladder
after the age of sixty.
I think of this, beneath him.

Seventy-six. And what if he falls?

Could I catch him in the barrow?
Should I, a young man, break his fall
across my back?

And next year, no one would stop the apples
rotting on the ground, and no one
would have heard the tree creaking all those autumns.

The barrow wheel turns over and not much is said.

Mr Kinder in Hospital

His winter garden misses him.
Two months three days from here,
they'll pull the apple tree down.
Fungus. Underground. Starts in roots.

Two hours six minutes from here,
the hospital's automatic doors will open
and your distances gape like a wide field
with a single stick driven into the ground.

Two hours eleven minutes from here,
you'll stand at the bus stop.
The rain that will fall on you there
is travelling now, on time.

Little Things

A walk was your idea; the foggy morning
the one place you found fit for a confession.

You were sick on the path, folded over your arm,
beneath the first crackling of rain. Outside the park,

birds spoke from aerials, made arrangements
with insects that waited for summer,

waited to come up from their heavy mud
and swim to an uncompromising light.

Midair

If it all goes wrong, midair,
I doubt I could put us down safely in a river.

I suspect I'd slam us nose first into the circuit board
of a densely populated suburb.

If I could, our rescue might be beamed across the globe;
stood on the wing as though we stood on water.

If it all goes wrong,
I doubt I could put us down.